W9-BZF-955

ANSWERS TO EXERCISES

IN

Third Edition

JANE E. AARON

AND

CAROL HOLLAR-ZWICK

PEARSON

Longman

New York   Boston   San Francisco
London   Toronto   Sydney   Tokyo   Singapore   Madrid
Mexico City   Munich   Paris   Cape Town   Hong Kong   Montreal

Executive Editor: Lynn Huddon
Senior Supplements Editor: Donna Campion
Electronic Page Makeup: Grapevine Publishing Services, Inc.

Answers to Exercises in LB Brief, Third Edition, by Jane E. Aaron and Carol Hollar-Zwick.

Copyright © 2008 by Pearson Education, Inc.

All rights reserved. Printed in the United States of America. Instructors may reproduce portions of this book for classroom use only. All other reproductions are strictly prohibited without prior permission of the publisher, except in the case of brief quotations embodied in critical articles and reviews.

Please visit the *LB Brief* Web site at *http://www.ablongman.com/aaronlbbrief3e*.

ISBN: 0-205-54991-8

1 2 3 4 5 6 7 8 9 10—OPM—10 09 08 07

Preface

This booklet contains answers for the exercises in *LB Brief,* Third Edition. The answer key has several possible uses:

- Instructors can use it to check students' responses on homework and quizzes.
- Some or all answers may be duplicated for class discussions or conferences.
- Some or all answers may be duplicated so that students can work independently on the exercises.

The answers labeled in this booklet with an asterisk (*) are also provided in the back of the book itself. These answers may be used to stimulate discussion or to encourage independent student work.

Answers are labeled "possible" when the corresponding exercises allow for choice in responding and the given answers are but suggestions. Even for the objective exercises, which more often lend themselves to one response, some users may disagree with some answers. Usage is often flexible, and many rules allow interpretation. The answers here conform to the usage recommended in *LB Brief.*

Contents

4 Sentence Parts and Patterns

5 Punctuation

6 Spelling and Mechanics

7 Research and Documentation

ANSWERS TO EXERCISES

IN

LB Brief

Third Edition

1. The Writing Process

CHAPTER 1. THE WRITING SITUATION

Exercise 1.1, p. 4
Analyzing a writing situation

The assignment specifies the subject (the combinations of client, therapist, and theory that tend to make psychotherapy successful), the audience (the instructor and a "discussion group" of classmates), and the purpose (to explain and support a conclusion about the subject). It requires research into studies of psychotherapy. It specifies a length range and a deadline. It does not specify a format, but APA format could be assumed because the course is in psychology.

Exercise 1.2, p. 6
Narrowing subjects

Individual response.

Exercise 1.3, p. 7
Analyzing audience

Individual response.

Exercise 1.4, p. 10
Finding purpose in assignments

Individual response.

CHAPTER 2. INVENTION

Exercise 2.1, p. 15
Using freewriting, brainstorming, or clustering

Individual response.

Exercise 2.2, p. 17
Developing a topic

Individual response.

CHAPTER 3. THESIS AND ORGANIZATION

Exercise 3.1, p. 20
Evaluating thesis statements

1. The statement lacks unity because the two halves do not seem to relate to each other.
   Possible revision: We should channel our natural feelings of aggression toward constructive rather than destructive ends.

2. The statement needs to be more specific and significant: How is Islam misunderstood? So what?
   Possible revision: Americans' misconceptions about Islam—especially that it is fanatical and oppressive—contribute to global instability.

3. Good thesis statement: limited, specific, and unified.

4. Both *good manners* and *make our society work* need to be more specific.
   Possible revision: Courtesy between people makes human interaction smoother and more efficient.

5. The statement simply states a fact.
   Possible revision: The poem depicts motherhood as a saintly calling.

6. The sentence lacks unity because the first half is positive and unspecific while the second half is negative and specific. Making the first half specific and the contrast explicit would unify the sentence.

Possible revision: Television does have its virtues, such as educational programming for children, but mostly it offers adults mindless escape from their problems.

7. The sentence is not a claim but a statement of personal preference.
   Possible revision: Courses in American history engage students the most when they move beyond personalities and political events to focus on social change.

8. The sentence lacks unity because the impairment does not clearly relate to the suspension.
   Possible revision: Because they have demonstrated bad judgment and lack of control by driving while impaired, drunken drivers should receive mandatory suspensions of their licenses.

9. The claim is not specific: *Why* is business a good major?
   Possible revision: For many students, a business major provides the right mix of academic and practical content to smooth the route to a career.

10. The sentence makes not one claim but several. It needs to be limited.
    Possible revision: The state's divorce laws should be made stricter for couples who have children.

Exercise 3.2, p. 27
Organizing ideas

Possible answer

I. Fans resist [new general idea].
   A. Sports seasons are already too crowded for fans.
      1. Baseball, football, hockey, and basketball seasons already overlap.
      2. Fans have limited time to watch.
      3. Fans have limited money to pay for sports.
   B. Soccer is unfamiliar [new general idea].
      1. A lot of kids play soccer in school, but the game is still "foreign."
      2. Soccer rules are unfamiliar.
II. Backers resist [new general idea].
   A. Sports money goes where the money is.
      1. Soccer fans couldn't fill huge stadiums.
      2. Backers are concerned with TV contracts.

3. TV contracts almost matter more than live audiences.
4. American soccer fans are too few for TV interest.
B. Backers are wary of losing money on new ventures.
1. Failure of the US Football League was costly.
2. Previous attempts to start a pro soccer league failed.

CHAPTER 4. DRAFTING

Exercise 4.1, p. 30
Analyzing a first draft

Possible answers

Some significant differences between Ling's outline and her first draft:

In paragraph 1, Ling explicitly addressed the essay by M. Kadi.
In paragraph 2, she added an explanation of how the Internet allows anonymity.
In paragraph 3, she added a long example from her experience.
In paragraph 4, she omitted planned examples and focused on working out her larger ideas. (Her readers objected to the lack of examples.)

CHAPTER 5. REVISING AND EDITING

Exercise 5.1, p. 36
Analyzing a revised draft

Answers will vary.

Exercise 5.2, p. 46
Analyzing an essay

The numbers below match the question numbers in the exercise instruction.

1. The writer's purpose is primarily self-expression but also explanation.

2. The writer seems to conceive of her readers as other inexperienced workers like herself. She assumes the role of a confider, sharing a difficult experience. Her tone is straightforward yet strangely subdued when she tells of Mrs. King's tyranny. We sense from the beginning that the writer was humbled by her experience, and the last paragraph is genuinely humble in tone.

3. The thesis statement (the last sentence of paragraph 1) clearly and specifically states the writer's topic (a work experience) and her perspective on that topic (learning something valuable).

4. The essay's organization is clearly chronological. The writer adheres to the organization throughout, providing ample signals to help the reader follow the narrative (e.g., *Last May, then, as soon as I arrived*).

5. This otherwise competent essay is marred by omissions of concrete details and examples that would give the reader a sense of actually sharing the experience instead of rushing through it. Paragraph 2: What did Mrs. King look like? How huge were the mail shipments? Paragraph 3: What were some of the actual words spoken by the writer and Mrs. King? Paragraph 4: What was inefficient about delivery routes and times for coffee breaks? What exactly did Mrs. King do or say in reacting to the writer's questions? Paragraph 5: In what specific ways did the writer pester Mrs. King? How were the efforts fruitless? How counterproductive? What snide names did Mrs. King use? How did she pick on the writer's work? What reprimands did she issue?

6. Individual response.

CHAPTER 6. PARAGRAPHS

Exercise 6.1, p. 51
Revising a paragraph for unity

The topic sentence is sentence 1. Unrelated are sentences 4 and 7.

Exercise 6.2, p. 51
Writing a unified paragraph

Delete statements not pertaining to Mozart's accomplishments: when he was born, where he lived, when he married, his debts. Possible paragraph:

Mozart's accomplishments in music seem remarkable even today. At the age of six he made his first concert tour of Europe, playing harpsichord, organ, and violin. He had begun composing music at the age of five, and by adolescence he had published numerous musical compositions. When he died at thirty-five, his work included over six hundred compositions, most notably operas, symphonies, quartets, and piano concertos.

Exercise 6.3, p. 51
Turning topic sentences into unified paragraphs

Individual response.

Exercise 6.4, p. 57
Arranging sentences coherently

Possible answer

The coherent order would be 1, 2, 5, 3, 6, 4.

Exercise 6.5, p. 58
Analyzing paragraphs for coherence

1. Begas paragraph: Organization: chronological. Parallelism: *They persuaded . . . they deprived; Jill became . . . she dropped out.* Repetition: *lonely, college/school.* Pronouns: *Jill/she; men and women/they.* Transitional expressions: *Between . . . , increasingly, Before long, too.*
2. Dyson paragraph: Organization: climactic. Parallelism and repetition: *reason is the need . . . reason is the need . . . reason is our spiritual need.* Further repetition: *space, earth/this planet.* Pronouns: *we, our, us.* Transitional expressions: *first, second, third.*

Exercise 6.6, p. 58
Writing a coherent paragraph

Possible paragraph

Hypnosis is far superior to drugs for relieving tension. It is inexpensive even for people who have not mastered self-hypnosis, whereas drugs are expensive. It is nonaddictive, whereas drugs foster addiction. And most important, hypnosis has none of the dangerous side effects of drugs, such as weight loss or gain, illness, and even death.

Exercise 6.7, p. 65
Analyzing and revising skimpy paragraphs

Possible answers

1. Sentence 1 requires some expansion to explain *quality of communication*. Each of the next two sentences needs to be supported with specific examples of the two qualities named.
2. Sentences 2 and 3 should each be followed by at least two specific examples of gestures to make the writer's meaning concrete.

Exercise 6.8, p. 65
Writing with the patterns of development

Individual response.

Exercise 6.9, p. 69
Analyzing an introduction and conclusion

Possible answers

The introduction in the first draft rushes to Kadi's essay without first securing the reader's interest, and it summarizes and dismisses Kadi's point too tersely. In contrast, the final introduction approaches readers with a statement and question of general interest, more fully explains Kadi's point, and grants it some value.

The conclusion in the first draft is abrupt, does not pick up both of the essay's main points (becoming more tolerated as well as more tolerant), and does not clearly link tolerance to community. The final conclusion solves these problems (especially with the addition of common ground) and finishes strongly.

CHAPTER 7. DOCUMENT DESIGN

Exercise 7.1, p. 78
Redesigning a paper

Individual response.

2. Writing in and out of College

CHAPTER 8. ACADEMIC WRITING

Exercise 8.1, p. 91
Using academic language

Possible revision

The stereotype that women talk more on cell phones than men do turns out to be false. In a five-year survey of 1021 cell phone owners, a major wireless company found that men spend 35 percent more time on their phones. They talk an average of 571 minutes a month compared to women's average of 424 minutes a month. Women do talk more on home phones than men do, but that difference is declining.

Exercise 8.2, p. 91
Considering your academic writing

Individual response.

Exercise 8.3, p. 91
Considering your native language or dialect

Individual response.

CHAPTER 10. CRITICAL READING AND WRITING

Exercise 10.1, p. 106
Previewing an essay

Individual response.

Exercise 10.2, p. 109
Reading

Individual response.

Exercise 10.3, p. 110
Summarizing

Possible answer

As their support of the government's student loan program illustrates, politicians ignore the economic reality that using resources to benefit one group (students in debt) involves taking the resources from another group (taxpayers). Students' average debt is not even that high, and college graduates can afford to pay it off. The greatest attention is paid to the graduate with a large debt, but the law also allows affluent students to borrow, even if their parents profit and the students drop out of school or waste time there. Funded by taxpayers, the loan program has contributed to declining educational standards, rising tuitions, and rising professors' salaries. Taxpayers should balk at funding the program further.

Exercise 10.4, p. 112
Reading an essay critically

Individual response.

Exercise 10.5, p. 119
Viewing an image critically

Individual response.

Exercise 10.6, p. 119
Viewing an image critically

Individual response.

Exercise 10.7, p. 119
Viewing an image critically

Individual response.

Exercise 10.8, p. 122
Responding to critical writing

Individual response.

Exercise 10.9, p. 122
Writing critically about a text

Individual response.

Exercise 10.10, p. 122
Writing critically about an image

Individual response.

Exercise 10.11, p. 122
Writing critically about an image

Individual response.

Exercise 10.12, p. 123
Writing critically about an image

Individual response.

CHAPTER 11. WRITING ARGUMENTS

Exercise 11.1, p. 124
Testing argument subjects

Subjects that are not appropriate for argument:

  2. A matter of facts, and few people would disagree.
  4. A matter of facts, and few people would disagree.
  8. A matter of personal preference.
  9. A matter of facts.
 10. A matter of personal belief.

Exercise 11.2, p. 125
Conceiving a thesis statement

Possible answers

Thesis statements for appropriate subjects in Exercise 11.1:

  1. An athletic scholarship should be what the term implies: an award
      to one who is both a superior athlete and a superior scholar.

3. Although censoring the Web sites of hate groups might offer some protection to persecuted groups or individuals, such censorship would be far too costly to free speech.

5. Until the city can construct private housing for the homeless, it must do more to make public shelters safe and clean.

6. Billboards help to destabilize urban neighborhoods by creating the impression that the neighborhoods are mere roadways.

7. Humane testing methods are adequate enough that cosmetics companies do not have to abuse animals in testing.

Exercise 11.3, p. 126
Using evidence

Individual response.

Exercise 11.4, p. 132
Reasoning inductively

The unreasonable generalizations from the given evidence are statements 2 (can't be inferred from the facts), 3 (contradicted by the facts), and 5 (can't be inferred from the facts).

Exercise 11.5, p. 132
Reasoning deductively

Possible answers

*1. Premise: Anyone who has opposed pollution controls may continue to do so.
   Premise: The mayor has opposed pollution controls.
   Conclusion: The mayor may continue to do so.
   The statement is valid and true.

*2. Premise: Corporate Web sites are sponsored by for-profit entities.
   Premise: Information from for-profit entities is unreliable.
   Conclusion: Information on corporate Web sites is unreliable.
   The statement is untrue because the second premise is untrue.

3. Premise: Many good artists trained at Parsons.
   Premise: Schroeder trained at Parsons.
   Conclusion: Schroeder is a good artist.
   The statement is invalid because the first premise does not necessarily apply to the second.

4. Premise: Those who use their resources to help others deserve our particular appreciation.

Premise: Some wealthy athletes use their resources to help others.
Conclusion: Some wealthy athletes deserve our particular appreciation.
The statement is valid and, if the first premise is accepted, true.

5. Premise: Any employer who has hired only one woman is sexist.
   Premise: Jimson is an employer who has hired only one woman.
   Conclusion: Jimson is sexist.
   The statement is untrue because the first premise is not true: there
   may be other reasons besides sexism for hiring only one woman.

Exercise 11.6, p. 133
Identifying appeals

Possible answers

*1. Primarily emotional appeal. Ethical appeal: knowledgeable,
    concerned, reasonable (at least in the two uses of *may*), slightly
    sarcastic (*most essential of skills*).
*2. Primarily rational appeal. Ethical appeal: knowledgeable, reasonable.
 3. Primarily rational appeal. Ethical appeal: knowledgeable, fair,
    willing to acknowledge opposing views.
 4. Primarily emotional appeal. Ethical appeal: sympathetic toward
    animals (but perhaps unfair to *so-called scientists*).
 5. Primarily rational appeal. Ethical appeal: knowledgeable, fair,
    willing to acknowledge opposing views.

Exercise 11.7, p. 133
Reaching your readers

Individual response.

Exercise 11.8, p. 137
Identifying and revising fallacies

Possible answers

*1. Sweeping generalization and begged question.
    A revision: A successful marriage demands a degree of maturity.
*2. Hasty generalization and non sequitur.
    A revision: Students' persistent complaints about the unfairness of the
    grading system should be investigated.
*3. Reductive fallacy.
    A revision: The United States got involved in World War II for
    many complex reasons. The bombing of Pearl Harbor was a
    triggering incident.

*4. Either/or fallacy and hasty generalization.

   A revision: People watch television for many reasons, but some watch because they are too lazy to talk or read or because they want mindless escape from their lives.

*5. Reductive fallacy and begged question.

   A revision: Racial tension may occur when people with different backgrounds live side by side.

6. Sweeping generalization and begged question (of the possibility/ likelihood that emerged nations can/will convert nuclear energy to nuclear bombs).

   A revision: If they are allowed to have it for creating energy, some emerging nations might put nuclear technology to work in bombs.

7. Post hoc fallacy.

   A revision: My cousin's experience of blacking out three times after climbing Pikes Peak once again shows that more research is needed into the aftereffects of mountain climbing.

8. Either/or fallacy.

   A revision: Failing to promote democracy throughout the Middle East could weaken American influence in the region.

9. Non sequitur.

   A revision: She admits to being an atheist, so how could she be a good Sunday school teacher?

10. Begged question.

   A revision: For most teenagers, who are vulnerable to peer pressure and experienced with sex, abstinence is a better choice than contraceptives.

Exercise 11.9, p. 137
Analyzing advertisements

Individual response.

Exercise 11.10, p. 138
Identifying fallacies online

Individual response.

Exercise 11.11, p. 139
Organizing your argument

Individual response.

3. Clarity and Style

CHAPTER 15. EMPHASIS

Exercise 15.1, p. 178
Revising: Emphasis of subjects and verbs

Possible answers

*1. Many <u>heroes helped</u> to emancipate the slaves.
*2. <u>Harriet Tubman</u>, an escaped slave herself, <u>guided</u> hundreds of other slaves to freedom on the Underground Railroad.

3. <u>Tubman risked</u> a return to slavery or possibly death.
4. During the Civil War <u>she also carried</u> information from the South to the North.
5. After the war, <u>Tubman raised</u> money to help needy former slaves.

Exercise 15.2, p. 180
Sentence combining: Beginnings and endings

Possible answers

*1. Pat Taylor strode into the <u>packed room</u>, greeting students called "Taylor's Kids" and nodding to their parents and teachers.
*2. This wealthy Louisiana oilman <u>had promised his "Kids" free college educations</u> because he was determined to make higher education available to all qualified but disadvantaged students.

3. The students <u>welcomed Taylor</u>, their voices singing "You Are the Wind Beneath My Wings," their faces flashing with self-confidence.
4. <u>They had thought a college education was beyond their dreams</u>, seeming too costly and too demanding.
5. To help ease the costs and demands of getting to college, <u>Taylor created a bold plan</u> of scholarships, tutoring, and counseling.

Exercise 15.3, p. 183
Revising: Excessive or faulty coordination

Possible answers

*1. Because soldiers admired their commanding officers, they often gave them nicknames containing the word *old*, even though not all of the commanders were old.

*2. General Thomas "Stonewall" Jackson was also called "Old Jack," although he was not yet forty years old.

3. Another Southern general, whose full name was James Longstreet, was called "Old Pete."

4. The Union general Henry W. Halleck had a reputation as a good military strategist, and he was an expert on the work of a French military authority, Henri Jomini. Therefore, Halleck was called "Old Brains."

5. After General William Henry Harrison won a victory at the Battle of Tippecanoe, he received the nickname "Old Tippecanoe." He used the name in his presidential campaign slogan, "Tippecanoe and Tyler, Too." Although he won the election in 1840, he died of pneumonia a month after taking office.

Exercise 15.4, p. 186
Revising: Faulty or excessive subordination

Possible answers

*1. Genaro González is a successful writer whose stories and novels have been published to critical acclaim.

*2. Although he loves to write, he has also earned a doctorate in psychology.

3. His first story, titled "Un Hijo del Sol," reflects his growing consciousness of his Aztec heritage and place in the world.

4. González writes equally well in English and Spanish. He received a large fellowship enabling him to take a leave of absence from the University of Texas–Pan American, where he teaches psychology, so that he could write without worrying about an income.

5. González wrote the first version of "Un Hijo del Sol" while he was a sophomore at Pan American. The university is in the Rio Grande valley of southern Texas, which González calls "el Valle" in the story.

Exercise 15.5, p. 186
Revising: Coordination and subordination

Possible revision

*Sir Walter Raleigh personified the Elizabethan Age, the period of Elizabeth I's rule of England, in the last half of the sixteenth century. *Raleigh was a courtier, a poet, an explorer, and an entrepreneur. *Supposedly, he gained Queen Elizabeth's favor by throwing his cloak beneath her feet at the right moment, just as she was about to step over a puddle. Although there is no evidence for this story, it illustrates Raleigh's dramatic and dynamic personality. His energy drew others to him, and he was one of Elizabeth's favorites. She supported him and dispensed favors to him. However, he lost his queen's goodwill when without her permission he seduced and eventually married one of her maids of honor. After Elizabeth died, her successor, James I, imprisoned Raleigh in the Tower of London on false charges of treason. Raleigh was released after thirteen years but arrested again two years later on the old treason charges. At the age of sixty-six he was beheaded.

CHAPTER 16. PARALLELISM

Exercise 16.1, p. 190
Revising: Parallelism

Possible answers

*1. The ancient Greeks celebrated four athletic contests: the Olympic Games at Olympia, the Isthmiam Games near Corinth, the Pythian Games at Delphi, and the Nemean Games at Cleonae.
*2. Each day of the games consisted of either athletic events or ceremonies and sacrifices to the gods.
*3. In the years between the games, competitors were taught wrestling, javelin throwing, and boxing.
*4. Competitors ran sprints, participated in spectacular chariot and horse races, and ran long distances while wearing full armor.

*5. The purpose of such events was developing physical strength, demonstrating skill and endurance, and <u>sharpening</u> the skills needed for war.

6. Events were held <u>both for</u> men and for boys.

7. At the Olympic Games the spectators cheered their favorites to victory, attended sacrifices to the gods, <u>and feasted</u> on the meat not burned in offerings.

8. The athletes competed less to achieve great wealth than <u>to gain</u> honor <u>for both</u> themselves and their cities.

9. Of course, exceptional athletes received financial support from patrons, poems and statues by admiring artists, and <u>even lavish</u> living quarters from their sponsoring cities.

10. With the medal counts and flag ceremonies, today's Olympians sometimes seem to be proving their countries' superiority more than <u>demonstrating</u> individual talent.

Exercise 16.2, p. 190
Sentence combining: Parallelism

Possible answers

*1. People can develop post-traumatic stress disorder (PTSD) after experiencing a dangerous situation and fearing for their survival.

*2. The disorder can be triggered by a wide variety of events, such as combat, a natural disaster, or a hostage situation.

3. PTSD can occur immediately after the stressful incident or not until many years later.

4. Sometimes people with PTSD will act irrationally and angrily.

5. Other symptoms include dreaming that one is reliving the experience, hallucinating that one is back in the terrifying place, and imagining that strangers are actually one's former torturers.

CHAPTER 17. VARIETY AND DETAILS

Exercise 17.1, p. 195
Revising: Variety

Possible revision

*<u>After being</u> dormant for many years, the Italian volcano Vesuvius exploded on August 24 in the year AD 79. *The ash, pumice, and mud

from the volcano buried two towns—Herculaneum and the more famous Pompeii—which lay undiscovered until 1709 and 1748, respectively. The excavation of Pompeii was the more systematic, the occasion for initiating modern methods of conservation and restoration. Whereas Herculaneum was simply looted of its most valuable finds and then left to disintegrate, Pompeii appears much as it did during the eruption. A luxurious house opens onto a lush central garden. An election poster decorates a wall. And a dining table is set for breakfast.

CHAPTER 18. APPROPRIATE AND EXACT WORDS

Exercise 18.1, p. 202
Revising: Appropriate words

Possible answers

*1. Acquired immune deficiency syndrome (AIDS) is a serious threat all over the world.

*2. The disease is transmitted primarily by sexual intercourse, exchange of bodily fluids, shared needles, and blood transfusions.

*3. Those who think the disease is limited to homosexuals, drug users, and foreigners are quite mistaken.

*4. Statistics suggest that in the United States one in every five hundred college students carries the HIV virus that causes AIDS.

*5. People with HIV or full-blown AIDS do not deserve others' exclusion or callousness. Instead, they need all the compassion, medical care, and financial assistance due the seriously ill.

6. A person with HIV or AIDS often sees a team of doctors or a single doctor with a specialized practice.

7. The doctor may help patients by obtaining social services for them as well as by providing medical care.

8. The person with HIV or AIDS who loses his or her job may need public assistance.

9. For someone who is very ill, a home-care nurse may be necessary. The nurse can administer medications and make the sick person as comfortable as possible.

10. Some people with HIV or AIDS have insurance, but others lack the money for premiums.

Exercise 18.2, p. 202
Revising: Sexist language

Possible answers

*1. When people apply for a job, they should represent themselves with the best possible résumé.
*2. A person applying for a job as a mail carrier should appear to be honest and responsible.
*3. Applicants for a position as an in-home nurse should also represent themselves as honest and responsible.
*4. Of course, the applicant should also have a background of capable nursing.
*5. The business executive who is scanning a stack of résumés will, of necessity, read them all quickly.

6. Applicants who want their résumés to stand out will make sure they highlight their best points.
7. Web designers will highlight their experience with computers.
8. Volunteer work may be appropriate, too, such as being chairperson [*or* chair] of a student organization.
9. If the student has been secretary for a campus organization, he or she could include that volunteer experience in the résumé.
10. If people writing résumés would keep in mind the people who will be reading them, applicants might know better what to include and how to format that information.

Exercise 18.3, p. 206
Using a dictionary

Answers will depend on the dictionary being consulted. Desk dictionaries disagree, for instance, over many of the syllable divisions. Thus no answers are provided.

Exercise 18.4, p. 206
Revising: Denotation

*1. Maxine Hong Kingston was awarded many prizes for her first two books, *The Woman Warrior* and *China Men.*
*2. Kingston cites her mother's tales about ancestors and ancient Chinese customs as the sources of these memoirs.

*3. Two of Kingston's <u>progenitors</u>, her great-grandfathers, are focal points of *China Men.*

*4. Both men led rebellions against <u>oppressive</u> employers: a sugarcane farmer and a railroad-construction engineer.

*5. In her childhood Kingston was greatly <u>affected</u> by her mother's tale about a pregnant aunt who was ostracized by villagers. [*Ostracized* is correct.]

6. The aunt gained <u>vengeance</u> by drowning herself in the village's water supply.

7. Kingston decided to make her nameless relative <u>famous</u> by giving her immortality in *The Woman Warrior.* [*Immortality* is correct.]

8. *Premier* is correct.

9. Both *embody* and *principles* are correct.

10. Kingston's innovative books <u>imply</u> her opposition to racism and sexism both in the China of the past and in the United States of the present.

Exercise 18.5, p. 207
Considering the connotations of words

*1. AIDS is a serious health <u>problem.</u>

*2. Once the virus has entered the blood system, it <u>destroys</u> T-cells.

3. The <u>function</u> of T-cells is to combat infections.

4. Without enough T-cells, the body is nearly <u>defenseless</u> against infections.

5. To prevent exposure to the disease, one should be especially <u>cautious</u> in sexual relationships.

Exercise 18.6, p. 208
Revising: Concrete and specific words

Possible revision

   I remember <u>as if it were last week</u> how <u>frightened</u> I felt the first time I <u>neared</u> Mrs. Murphy's second-grade class. <u>Just three days</u> before, I had moved from a <u>rural one-street</u> town in Missouri to a suburb of Chicago where the <u>houses and people were jammed together.</u> My new school looked <u>monstrous</u> from the outside and seemed <u>forbiddingly dim</u> inside as I walked haltingly down the endless corridor toward the classroom. The class was clamorous as I neared the door; but when I slipped inside, twenty faces became still and gawked at me. I felt terrified and longed for a place to hide. However, in a booming voice Mrs. Murphy ordered me to the front of the room to introduce myself.

Exercise 18.7, p. 210
Using prepositions in idioms

*1. As Mark and Lana waited for the justice of the peace, they seemed oblivious to [or of] the other people in the lobby.
*2. But Mark inferred from Lana's glance at a handsome man that she was no longer occupied by him alone.
 3. Angry with Lana, Mark charged her with not loving him enough to get married.
 4. Impatient at Mark's childish behavior, Lana disagreed with his interpretation of her glance.
 5. They decided that if they could differ so violently over a minor incident, they should part from each other.

Exercise 18.8, p. 211
Using prepositions in idioms

*1. The Eighteenth Amendment to the Constitution of the United States was ratified in 1919.
*2. It prohibited the "manufacture, sale, or transportation of intoxicating liquors."

 3. It was adopted in response to a nationwide crusade by temperance groups.
 4. The amendment did not prevent Americans from drinking, and the sale of alcoholic beverages was taken over by organized crime.
 5. Wide-scale smuggling and bootlegging came with the demand for liquor.

Exercise 18.9, p. 212
Using figurative language

Individual response.

Exercise 18.10, p. 213
Revising: Trite expressions

Possible answers

*1. The <u>disasters</u> of the war have shaken the small nation <u>severely</u>.
*2. Prices for food have <u>risen markedly</u>, and citizens <u>suspect</u> that others are <u>profiting</u> on the black market.
*3. Medical supplies are so <u>scarce</u> that even <u>very sick</u> civilians cannot get treatment.
*4. With most men fighting or injured or killed, women have had to take <u>men's places</u> in farming and manufacturing.
*5. <u>Finally</u>, the war's <u>high cost</u> has <u>destroyed the nation's economy</u>.

6. Our reliance on foreign oil to support our <u>many cars</u> has <u>peaked</u> in recent years.
7. Sport-utility vehicles, <u>which get low gas mileage</u>, are responsible for part of the increase.
8. In the near future, we may have to <u>make sacrifices, making</u> use of public transportation or <u>driving</u> more fuel-efficient cars.
9. Both solutions are <u>easy to propose</u> but <u>difficult to implement</u>.
10. But we <u>must acknowledge</u> that we cannot <u>continue to deplete</u> the world's oil reserves.

CHAPTER 19. COMPLETENESS

Exercise 19.1, p. 215
Revising: Completeness

Possible answers

*1. The first ice cream, eaten <u>in</u> China in about 2000 BC, was lumpier than modern ice cream.
*2. The Chinese made their ice cream of milk, spices, and overcooked rice and packed <u>it</u> in snow to solidify.

3. In the fourteenth century ice milk and fruit ices appeared in Italy and <u>on</u> the tables of the wealthy.
4. At <u>her</u> wedding in 1533 to the king of France, Catherine de Médicis offered several flavors <u>of</u> fruit ices.
5. Modern sherbets resemble her <u>ices</u>; modern ice cream <u>resembles</u> her soft dessert of thick, sweetened cream.

CHAPTER 20. CONCISENESS

Exercise 20.1, p. 221
Revising: Writing concisely

Possible answers

*1. If sore muscles after exercising are a problem for you, there are some things you can do to ease the discomfort.
*2. First, apply cold immediately to reduce inflammation.
*3. Cold constricts blood vessels and keeps blood away from the injured muscles.
*4. Avoid heat for the first day.
*5. Applying heat within the first twenty-four hours can increase muscle soreness and stiffness.

6. You can apply cold in two ways: with a cold shower or with an ice pack.
7. You can also reduce muscle inflammation with aspirin, ibuprofen, or another anti-inflammatory medication.
8. Muscle soreness can be worsened by power lifting.
9. While healing occurs, you need to rest.
10. A day or two after overdoing exercise, you can get some light exercise and gentle massage.

Exercise 20.2, p. 221
Revising: Conciseness

Possible answers

*After much thought, he concluded that carcinogens could be treated like automobiles. *Instead of giving in to a fear of cancer, we should balance the benefits we receive from potential carcinogens (such as plastic and pesticides) against the damage they do. Similarly, instead of responding irrationally to the pollution caused by automobiles, we have decided to live with them and enjoy their benefits while simultaneously working to improve them.

4. Sentence Parts and Patterns

CHAPTER 21. PARTS OF SPEECH

Exercise 21.1, p. 228
Identifying nouns, pronouns, and verbs

     N   N   N   N   N
*1. Ancestors of the ginkgo tree, a relic from the age of the dinosaurs,
   V   N
    lived 175 to 200 million years ago.
       N   V   N   N
*2. The tree sometimes grows to over a hundred feet in height.
    P V   N   N
*3. It has fan-shaped leaves about three inches wide.
        N   N   V P N   N   P
*4. A deciduous tree, the ginkgo loses its leaves in the fall after they
    V
    turn bright yellow.
          N V   N   N
*5. The ginkgo tree is esteemed in the United States and Europe as an
       N
    ornamental tree.

             N   V   N   N   N
6. Because the ginkgo shows tolerance for smoke, low temperatures,
       N   P   V   N
   and low rainfall, it appears in many cities.
      N   V   N   P N
7. A shortcoming, however, is the foul odor of its fruit.
      N   N   V   N
8. The fruit of the ginkgo looks something like a plum.
       N V   N   N   V
9. Inside the fruit lies a large white seed that some Asians value as a
   N
   food.
                   N   V N   N V
10. Because only the female ginkgo bears fruit, the male is more
                  N
    common as an ornamental tree.

Exercise 21.2, p. 229
Identifying adjectives and adverbs

             ADJ ADJ ADJ
*1. You can reduce stress by making a few simple changes.

    ADV ADJ   ADV   ADV
*2. Get up fifteen minutes earlier than you ordinarily do.

    ADJ ADJ   ADV
*3. Eat a healthy breakfast, and eat it slowly so that you enjoy it.

         ADJ   ADV   ADJ
*4. Do your unpleasant tasks early in the day.

    ADJ   ADJ   ADV
*5. Every day, do at least one thing you really enjoy.

                   ADJ   ADJ
6. If waiting in lines is stressful for you, carry a book or magazine

    when you know you'll have to wait.

                   ADV   ADV
7. Make promises sparingly and keep them faithfully.

        ADV   ADJ
8. Plan ahead to prevent stressful situations.

             ADJ   ADJ
9. For example, carry spare keys so you won't be locked out of your

    car or house.

       ADJ   ADJ   ADV
10. See a doctor and a dentist regularly.

Exercise 21.3, p. 231
Adding connecting words

  *1. Just about everyone has heard the story of the Trojan Horse.

  *2. This incident happened at the city of Troy and was planned by the Greeks.

  *3. The Greeks built a huge wooden horse; inside it was a hollow space big enough to hold many men.

  *4. At night, they rolled the horse to the gate of Troy and left it there before sailing their ships out to sea.

  *5. In the morning, the Trojans were surprised to see the enormous horse.

  6. But they were amazed when they saw that the Greeks were gone.

  7. Because they were curious to examine this gift from the Greeks, they dragged the horse into the city and left it outside the temple.

8. In the middle of the night, the hidden Greeks emerged <u>from</u> the horse and began setting fires all over town.
9. <u>When</u> the Trojan soldiers awoke and came out of their houses, the Greeks killed them one by one.
10. By the next morning, the Trojan men were dead <u>and</u> the women were slaves to the Greeks.

CHAPTER 22. THE SENTENCE

Exercise 22.1, p. 234
Identifying subjects and predicates

*1. The <u>horse</u> | <u>has</u> a long history of serving humanity but today <u>is</u> mainly a <u>show</u> and sport animal.
*2. A member of the genus *Equus*, the domestic <u>horse</u> | <u>is related</u> to the wild Przewalski's horse, the ass, and the zebra.
*3. The domestic <u>horse</u> and its <u>relatives</u> | <u>are</u> all plains-dwelling herd animals.
*4. An average-sized adult <u>horse</u> | <u>may require</u> twenty-six pounds or more of pasture feed or hay per day.
*5. <u>Racehorses</u> | <u>require</u> grain for part of their forage.

6. Oddly, the modern <u>horse</u> | <u>evolved</u> in North America and then became extinct here after spreading to other parts of the world.
7. <u>It</u> | <u>was reintroduced</u> here by the Spaniards, profoundly affecting the culture of Native Americans.
8. The North American <u>animals</u> called wild horses | <u>are</u> actually <u>descended</u> from escaped domesticated horses that reproduced in the wild.
9. According to records, <u>horses</u> | <u>were hunted</u> and <u>domesticated</u> as early as four to five thousand years ago.
10. The earliest <u>ancestor</u> of the modern horse | <u>may have been</u> eohippus, approximately 55 million years ago.

Exercise 22.2, p. 237
Identifying sentence parts

               S   V
*1. The number of serious crimes in the United States decreased.

        S   V
*2. A decline in serious crimes occurred each year.

        S   V   DO
*3. The Crime Index measures serious crime.

        S   V   DO
*4. The FBI invented the index.

                                    S   V   SC   SC   SC
*5. The four serious violent crimes are murder, robbery, forcible rape,

               SC
    and aggravated assault.

        S   S   S   S   V
6. Auto theft, burglary, arson, and larceny-theft are the four serious

     SC
    crimes against property.

        S   V   IO   DO
7. The Crime Index gives the FBI a measure of crime.

        S   V   DO
8. The index shows trends in crimes and criminals.

                     S   V   DO
9. The nation's largest cities showed the largest decline in crime.

                     S   V   DO   OC
10. Their crime-fighting success made some cities models for others.

Exercise 22.3, p. 240
Rewriting passives and expletives

*1. <u>Milo Addica and Will Rokos</u> <u>cowrote</u> the screenplay for *Monster's
    Ball.*

*2. <u>Marc Foster</u> <u>directed</u> the film.

3. <u>Only one performance</u> in the movie <u>received</u> an Academy Award.

4. <u>Halle Berry</u> <u>won</u> the award for best actress.

5. <u>The press</u> <u>congratulated</u> Berry for being the first African American
   to win the award.

CHAPTER 23. PHRASES AND SUBORDINATE CLAUSES

Exercise 23.1, p. 244
Identifying phrases

                                     appositive phrase
            prepositional phrase   prepositional phrase
*1. Because of its many synonyms, or words with similar meanings,

                        infinitive phrase
English can make it difficult to choose the exact word.

                       participial phrase
             prepositional phrase   appositive phrase
*2. Borrowing words from other languages such as French and Latin,

                      prepositional
                      phrase
English acquired an unusual number of synonyms.

         participial phrase   prepositional phrase
*3. Having so many choices, how does a writer decide between *motherly*

                        prepositional phrase
and *maternal* or among *womanly, feminine,* and *female*?

                                    infinitive phrase
*4. Some people prefer longer and more ornate words to avoid the

               prepositional phrase
flatness of short words.

                                      prepositional phrase
        prepositional phrase   participle
*5. During the Renaissance a heated debate occurred between the

                      prepositional phrase
         participial phrase   participial phrase
Latinists, favoring Latin words, and the Saxonists, preferring native

  prepositional phrase
Anglo-Saxon words.

              prepositional phrase
               participle   infinitive phrase
6. Students in writing classes are often told to choose the shorter word,

              appositive phrase
generally an Anglo-Saxon derivative.

7. Better advice, wrote William Hazlitt, is the principle of choosing

          ┌─ prepositional phrase ─
          │ ┌─gerund phrase ─

           ┌─ prepositional phrase ─┐
"the best word in common use."

     ┌────── participial phrase ──────┐
     │   ┌prepositional┐
     │   phrase
8. Keeping this principle in mind, a writer would choose either

        ┌──── appositive phrase ────┐   ┌──── appositive phrase ───┐
womanly, the Anglo-Saxon word, or *feminine*, a French derivative,

      ┌────── prepositional phrase ──────┐
according to meaning and situation.

                               ┌absolute phrase ─
9. Synonyms rarely have exactly the same meaning, usage having

defined differences.

                appositive
10. The Old English word *handbook*, for example, has a slightly different

      ┌   ── prepositional phrase ──────┐ ┌─ appositive phrase ─┐
                             appositive
meaning from the French derivative *manual*, a close synonym.

Exercise 23.2, p. 246
Identifying clauses

                           ADJ
*1. The Prophet Muhammad, <u>who was the founder of Islam</u>, was born

about 570 CE in the city of Mecca.

                                   ADV
*2. He grew up in the care of his grandfather and an uncle <u>because

both of his parents had died.</u>

                                   ADJ
*3. His family was part of a powerful Arab tribe <u>that lived in western

Arabia.</u>

                   ADV
*4. <u>When he was about forty years old</u>, he had a vision in a cave outside

Mecca.

                               N
*5. He believed <u>that God had selected him to be the prophet of a true

religion for the Arab people.</u>

6. Throughout his life he continued to have revelations, which have
   (ADJ)
   been written in the Koran.

7. The Koran is the sacred book of the Muslims, who as adherents of
   (ADJ)
   Islam view Muhammad as God's messenger.

8. When he no longer had the support of the clans of Mecca,
   (ADV)
   Muhammad and his followers moved to Medina.

9. There they established an organized Muslim community that
   (ADJ)
   sometimes clashed with the Meccans and with Jewish clans.

10. Throughout his life Muhammad continued as the religious,
    political, and military leader of Islam as it spread in Asia
    (ADV)
    and Africa.

CHAPTER 24. SENTENCE TYPES

Exercise 24.1, p. 248
Identifying sentence structures

*1. ⌈————— main clause —————⌉ ⌈————— main clause —————⌉
   Our world has many sounds, but they all have one thing in
   common. [*Compound.*]

*2. ⌈————————————— main clause —————————————⌉
   The one thing that all sounds share is that they are produced by
   ⌊— subordinate clause —⌋ ⌊— subordinate clause —⌋
   vibrations. [*Complex.*]

*3. ⌈————————— main clause —————————⌉ ⌈——— main clause ———
   The vibrations make the air move in waves, and these sound waves
   travel to the ear. [*Compound.*]

*4. ⌈————— subordinate clause —————⌉ ⌈————— main clause —————⌉
   When sound waves enter the ear, the brain has to interpret them.
   [*Complex.*]

*5. ⌈————————————— main clause —————————————⌉
   Sound waves can also travel through other material, such as water
   and even the solid earth. [*Simple.*]

main clause   main clause

6. Some sounds are pleasant, and others, which we call noise, are not.
   [*Compound-complex.*]
   subordinate clause

main clause

7. Most noises are produced by irregular vibrations at irregular
   main clause
   intervals; an example is the barking of a dog. [*Compound.*]

main clause

8. Sounds have frequency and pitch. [*Simple.*]

subordinate clause   main clause

9. When an object vibrates rapidly, it produces high-frequency, high-
   pitched sounds. [*Complex.*]

main clause

10. People can hear sounds over a wide range of frequencies; dogs and
    main clause
    cats can hear sounds with higher frequencies. [*Compound.*]

CHAPTER 25. VERB FORMS

Exercise 25.1, p. 253
Using irregular verbs

*1. The world population has <u>grown</u> by two-thirds of a billion people
   in less than a decade. [Past participle.]

*2. Recently it <u>broke</u> the 6 billion mark. [Past tense.]

*3. Experts have <u>drawn</u> pictures of a crowded future. [Past participle.]

*4. They predict that the world population may have <u>slid</u> up to as
   much as 10 billion by the year 2050. [Past participle.]

*5. Though the food supply <u>rose</u> in the last decade, the share to each
   person <u>fell</u>. [Both past tense.]

6. At the same time the water supply, which had actually <u>become</u>
   healthier in the twentieth century, <u>sank</u> in size and quality. [Past
   participle; past tense.]

7. The number of species on earth <u>shrank</u> by 20 percent. [Past tense.]

8. Changes in land use <u>ran</u> nomads and subsistence farmers off the
   land. [Past tense.]

9. Yet all has not been <u>lost</u>. [Past participle.]

10. Recently human beings have <u>begun</u> to heed these and other
    problems and to explore how technology can be <u>driven</u> to help the
    earth and all its populations. [Both past participles.]

11. Some new techniques for waste processing have <u>proved</u> [or <u>proven</u>] effective. [Past participle.]
12. Crop management has <u>taken</u> some pressure off lands with poor soil, allowing their owners to produce food. [Past participle.]
13. Genetic engineering could replenish food supplies that have <u>shrunk</u>. [Past participle.]
14. Population control has <u>found</u> adherents all over the world. [Past participle.]
15. Many endangered species have been <u>given</u> room to thrive. [Past participle.]

Exercise 25.2, p. 254
Distinguishing between *sit/set, lie/lay, rise/raise*

*1. Yesterday afternoon the child <u>lay</u> down for a nap.
*2. The child has been <u>raised</u> by her grandparents.

3. Most days her grandfather has <u>sat</u> with her, reading her stories.
4. She has <u>risen</u> at dawn most mornings.
5. Her toys were <u>laid</u> on the floor.

Exercise 25.3, p. 256
Using *-s* and *-ed* verb endings

*1. A teacher sometimes <u>asks</u> too much of a student.
*2. In high school I was once <u>punished</u> for being sick.
*3. I had <u>missed</u> a week of school because of a serious case of the flu.
*4. I <u>realized</u> that I would fail a test unless I had a chance to make up the class work.
*5. I <u>discussed</u> the problem with the teacher.

6. He said I was <u>supposed</u> to make up the work while I was sick.
7. At that I <u>walked</u> out of the class.
8. I <u>received</u> a failing grade then, but it did not change my attitude.
9. I <u>work</u> harder in the courses that have more understanding teachers.
10. Today I still balk when a teacher <u>makes</u> unreasonable demands or <u>expects</u> miracles.

Exercise 25.4, p. 261
Using helping verbs

*1. Each year thousands of new readers <u>have</u> been discovering Agatha Christie's mysteries.
*2. The books <u>were</u> written by a prim woman who had worked as a nurse during <u>World</u> War I.

3. Christie never expected that her play *The Mousetrap* <u>would</u> be performed for decades.
4. During her life Christie <u>was</u> always complaining about movie versions of her stories.
5. Readers of her stories <u>have</u> been delighted to be baffled by her.

Exercise 25.5, p. 261
Revising: Helping verbs plus main verbs

*1. A report from the Bureau of the Census has <u>confirmed</u> a widening gap between rich and poor.
*2. As suspected, the percentage of people below the poverty level did <u>increase</u> over the last decade.

3. More than 17 percent of the population is <u>making</u> 5 percent of all the income.
4. About 1 percent of the population will <u>be</u> keeping [*or* will <u>keep</u>] an average of $500,000 apiece after taxes.
5. Sentence correct.

Exercise 25.6, p. 264
Revising: Verbs plus gerunds or infinitives

*1. A program called HELP Wanted tries to encourage citizens <u>to</u> take action on behalf of American competitiveness.
*2. Officials working on this program hope <u>to improve</u> education for work.

3. American businesses find that their workers need <u>to learn</u> to read.
4. In the next ten years the United States expects <u>to face</u> a shortage of 350,000 scientists.
5. Sentence correct.

Exercise 25.7, p. 266
Revising: Verbs plus particles

*1. American movies treat everything from going out with [correct] someone to making up [correct] an ethnic identity, but few people look into their significance.

*2. While some viewers stay away from [correct] topical films, others turn up at the theater simply because a movie has sparked debate.

3. Some movies attracted rowdy spectators, and the theaters had to throw them out.

4. Filmmakers have always been eager to point their influence out [correct; *or* point out their influence] to the public.

5. Everyone agrees that filmmakers will keep on creating controversy, if only because it can fill up [correct] theaters.

CHAPTER 26. VERB TENSES

Exercise 26.1, p. 271
Revising: Consistent past tense

*The 1960 presidential race between Richard Nixon and John F. Kennedy was the first to feature a televised debate. [Sentence correct.] *Despite his extensive political experience, Nixon perspired heavily and looked haggard and uneasy in front of the camera. *By contrast, Kennedy projected cool poise and provided crisp answers that made him seem fit for the office of President. The public responded positively to Kennedy's image. [Sentence correct.] His poll ratings shot up immediately, while Nixon's took a corresponding drop. Kennedy won the election by a close 118,564 votes. [Sentence correct.]

Exercise 26.2, p. 271
Revising: Consistent present tense

*E. B. White's famous children's novel *Charlotte's Web* is a wonderful story of friendship and loyalty. [Sentence correct.] *Charlotte, the wise and motherly spider, decides to save her friend Wilbur, the young and childlike pig, from being butchered by his owner. *She makes a plan to weave words into her web that describe Wilbur. She first weaves "Some

Pig" and later <u>presents</u> "Terrific," "Radiant," and "Humble." Her plan <u>succeeds</u> beautifully. She fools the humans into believing that Wilbur <u>is</u> a pig unlike any other, and Wilbur <u>lives</u>.

Exercise 26.3, p. 274
Adjusting tense sequence: Past or past perfect tense

*1. Diaries that Adolf Hitler <u>was supposed</u> to have written <u>had surfaced</u> in Germany.
*2. Many people <u>believed</u> that the diaries <u>were</u> authentic because a well-known historian <u>had declared</u> them so.

3. However, the historian's evaluation <u>was questioned</u> by other authorities, who <u>called</u> the diaries forgeries.
4. They <u>claimed</u>, among other things, that the paper <u>was</u> not old enough to have been used by Hitler.
5. Eventually, the doubters <u>won</u> the debate because they <u>had</u> the best evidence.

Exercise 26.4, p. 274
Revising: Tense sequence with conditional sentences

*1. When an athlete <u>turns</u> professional, he or she commits to a grueling regimen of mental and physical training.
*2. If athletes <u>were</u> less committed, they <u>would disappoint</u> teammates, fans, and themselves.
*3. If professional athletes <u>are</u> very lucky, they may play until age forty.
*4. Unless an athlete achieves celebrity status, he or she <u>will have</u> few employment choices after retirement.
*5. If professional sports <u>were</u> less risky, athletes <u>would have</u> longer careers and more choices after retirement.

6. If you think you <u>might be</u> exposed to the flu in the winter, you <u>should get</u> a flu shot.
7. If you are allergic to eggs, you <u>might have</u> an allergic reaction to the flu shot.
8. If you get the flu after having a flu shot, your illness <u>will be</u> milder.
9. If you had had a flu shot last year, you <u>might</u> [*or* would] <u>have</u> avoided the illness.
10. If you <u>were</u> not so afraid of shots, you <u>would</u> get a flu shot every year.

CHAPTER 27. VERB MOOD

Exercise 27.1, p. 276
Revising: Subjunctive mood

*1. If John Hawkins <u>had known</u> of all the dangerous side effects of smoking tobacco, would he have introduced the dried plant to England in 1565?
*2. Hawkins noted that if a Florida Indian man <u>were</u> to travel for several days, he <u>would smoke</u> tobacco to satisfy his hunger and thirst.

3. Early tobacco growers feared that their product would not gain acceptance unless it <u>were</u> perceived as healthful.
4. To prevent fires, in 1646 the General Court of Massachusetts passed a law requiring that colonists <u>smoke</u> tobacco only if they were five miles from any town.
5. To prevent decadence, in 1647 Connecticut passed a law mandating that one's smoking of tobacco <u>be</u> limited to once a day in one's own home.

CHAPTER 28. VERB VOICE

Exercise 28.1, p. 279
Revising: Using the active voice

Possible answers

*1. Many <u>factors</u> <u>determine</u> water quality.
*2. All natural <u>waters</u> <u>contain</u> suspended and dissolved substances.
*3. The <u>environment</u> <u>controls</u> the amounts of the substances.
*4. <u>Pesticides</u> <u>produce</u> some dissolved substances.
*5. <u>Fields, livestock feedlots</u>, and other <u>sources</u> <u>deposit</u> sediment in water.

6. <u>Sediment</u> <u>affects</u> the bottom life of streams and lakes.
7. <u>Sediment</u> <u>reduces</u> light penetration, and the <u>lack of light</u> <u>may smother</u> bottom-dwelling organisms.
8. <u>Laboratories</u> frequently <u>measure</u> the quality of water in city systems.

9. If pollutants exceed legal levels, city officials must notify the citizens.
10. Many people dislike the chlorine taste of city water.

Exercise 28.2, p. 279
Converting between active and passive voices

Possible answers

*1. When engineers built the Eiffel Tower in 1889, the French thought it to be ugly.
*2. At the time, industrial technology was still resisted by many people.

3. This technology was typified by the tower's naked steel construction.
4. People expected beautiful ornament to grace fine buildings.
5. Further, people could not even call a structure without solid walls a building.

CHAPTER 29. AGREEMENT OF SUBJECT AND VERB

Exercise 29.1, p. 287
Revising: Subject-verb agreement

*1. Weinstein & Associates is a consulting firm that tries to make businesspeople laugh.
*2. Statistics from recent research suggest that humor relieves stress.
*3. Reduced stress in businesses in turn reduces illness and absenteeism.
*4. Reduced stress can also reduce friction within an employee group, which then works together more productively.
*5. In special conferences held by one consultant, each of the participants practices making others laugh.

6. "Aren't there enough laughs within you to spread the wealth?" the consultant asks his students.
7. Sentence correct.
8. Such self-deprecating comments in public are uncommon among business managers, the consultant says.
9. Each of the managers in a typical firm takes the work much too seriously.
10. The humorous boss often feels like the only one of the managers who has other things in mind besides profits.

11. One consultant to many companies suggests cultivating office humor with practical jokes such as a rubber fish in the water cooler.
12. When a manager or employees regularly post cartoons on the bulletin board, office spirit usually picks up.
13. Sentence correct.
14. In the face of levity, the former sourpuss becomes one of those who hide bad temper.
15. Every one of the consultants cautions, however, that humor has no place in life-affecting corporate situations such as employee layoffs.

Exercise 29.2, p. 287
Adjusting for subject-verb agreement

*The Siberian tiger is the largest living cat in the world, much bigger than its relative the Bengal tiger. *It grows to a length of nine to twelve feet, including its tail, and to a height of about three and a half feet. *It can weigh over six hundred pounds. *This carnivorous hunter lives in northern China and Korea as well as in Siberia. *During the long winter of this Arctic climate, the yellowish striped coat gets a little lighter in order to blend with the snow-covered landscape. *The coat also grows quite thick, since the tiger has to withstand temperatures as low as −50°F.

The Siberian tiger sometimes has to travel great distances to find food. It needs about twenty pounds of food a day because of its size and the cold climate, but when it has fresh food it may eat as much as a hundred pounds at one time. It hunts mainly deer, boars, and even bears, plus smaller prey such as fish and rabbits. It pounces on its prey and grabs it by the back of the neck. The animal that is not killed immediately is thrown to the ground and suffocated with a bite to the throat. Then the tiger feasts.

CHAPTER 30. PRONOUN CASE

Exercise 30.1, p. 292
Choosing between subjective and objective pronouns

*1. Jody and I had been hunting for jobs.
*2. The best employees at our old company were she and I, so we expected to find jobs quickly.

3. Between her and me the job search had lasted two months, and still it had barely begun.

4. Slowly, she and I stopped sharing leads.
5. It was obvious that Jody and I could not be as friendly as we had been.

Exercise 30.2, p. 293
Choosing between *who* and *whom*

*1. The school administrators suspended Jurgen, whom they suspected of setting the fire.
*2. Jurgen had been complaining to other custodians, who reported him.
*3. He constantly complained of unfair treatment from whoever happened to be passing in the halls, including pupils.
*4. "Who here has heard Mr. Jurgen's complaints?" the police asked.
*5. "Whom did he complain most about?"

6. His coworkers agreed that Jurgen seemed less upset with the staff or students, most of whom he did not even know, than with the building itself.
7. "He took out his aggression on the building," claimed one coworker who often witnessed Jurgen's behavior.
8. "He cursed and kicked the walls and whomever he saw nearby."
9. The coworker thought that Jurgen might have imagined people who instructed him to behave the way he did.
10. "He's someone whom other people can't get next to," said the coworker.

Exercise 30.3, p. 295
Revising: Pronoun case

*1. Sentence correct.
*2. Sentence correct.
*3. Immediately, he and Gilgamesh wrestled to see who was more powerful.
*4. Sentence correct.
*5. The friendship of the two strong men was sealed by their fighting.

6. Gilgamesh said, "Between you and me, mighty deeds will be accomplished, and our fame will be everlasting."
7. Among their glorious acts, Enkidu and he defeated a giant bull, Humbaba, and cut down the bull's cedar forests.
8. Sentence correct.

9. When Enkidu died, Gilgamesh mourned his death, realizing that no one had been a better friend than <u>he</u>.
10. When Gilgamesh himself died many years later, his people raised a monument praising Enkidu and <u>him</u> for their friendship and their mighty deeds of courage.

CHAPTER 31. AGREEMENT OF PRONOUN AND ANTECEDENT

Exercise 31.1, p. 300
Revising: Pronoun-antecedent agreement

Possible answers

*1. Each girl raised in a Mexican American family in the Rio Grande valley of Texas hopes that one day <u>she</u> will be given a *quinceañera* party for <u>her</u> fifteenth birthday.
*2. Such <u>a celebration is</u> very expensive because it entails a religious service followed by a huge party. *Or:* Such celebrations are very expensive because <u>they entail</u> a religious service followed by a huge party.
*3. A girl's immediate family, unless <u>it is</u> wealthy, cannot afford the party by <u>itself</u>.
*4. The parents will ask each close friend or relative if <u>he or she</u> can help with the preparations. *Or:* Her parents will ask <u>close friends or relatives</u> if they can help with the preparations.
*5. Sentence correct.

6. <u>Most children</u> will quickly astound observers with their capabilities. *Or:* Almost any child will quickly astound observers with <u>his or her</u> capabilities.
7. Sentence correct.
8. Of course, the family has a tremendous influence on the development of a child in <u>its</u> midst.
9. Each member of the immediate family exerts <u>his or her</u> own unique pull on the child.
10. Other relatives, teachers, and friends can also affect the child's view of the world and of <u>himself or herself</u>.
11. The workings of genetics also strongly influence the child, but <u>they</u> may never be fully understood.
12. Sentence correct.
13. Another debated issue is whether the child's emotional development or <u>his or her</u> intellectual development is more central.

14. Just about everyone has <u>his or her</u> strong opinion on these issues, often backed up by evidence.
15. Sentence correct.

CHAPTER 32. REFERENCE OF PRONOUN TO ANTECEDENT

Exercise 32.1, p. 304
Revising: Pronoun reference

Possible answers

*1. "Life begins at forty" is a cliché many people live by, and this <u>saying</u> may or may not be true.
*2. Living successfully or not depends on one's definition of <u>success</u>.
*3. When <u>Pearl Buck</u> was forty, <u>her</u> novel *The Good Earth* won the Pulitzer Prize.
*4. Buck was raised in a missionary family in China, <u>which</u> [*or* whom] she wrote about in her novels.
*5. In *The Good Earth* <u>the characters</u> have to struggle, but fortitude is rewarded.

6. Buck received much critical praise and earned over $7 million, but she was very modest about <u>her success</u> [*or* <u>the praise</u> *or* <u>the money</u>].
7. Pearl Buck donated most of her earnings to a foundation for Asian American children, <u>an act</u> that proves her generosity.
8. In the *Book of Romance* <u>a chapter is reserved</u> for the story of Elizabeth Barrett, who at forty married Robert Browning against her father's wishes.
9. In the 1840s <u>women</u> did not normally defy their fathers, but Elizabeth was too much in love to obey.
10. She left a poetic record of her love for Robert, and readers still enjoy reading <u>her poems</u>.

Exercise 32.2, p. 305
Revising: Pronoun reference

Possible revision

*In Charlotte Brontë's *Jane Eyre*, <u>Jane</u> is a shy young woman <u>who</u> takes a job as governess. *Her employer is a rude, brooding man named Rochester. [Sentence correct.] *He lives in a mysterious mansion on the

English moors, and both the mansion and the moors contribute an eerie quality to Jane's experience. *Eerier still are the fires, strange noises, and other unexplained happenings in the house; but Rochester refuses to discuss them. Eventually, Jane and Rochester fall in love. On the day they are to be married, however, Jane learns that Rochester has a wife hidden in the house. The wife is hopelessly insane and violent and must be guarded at all times, circumstances that explain Rochester's strange behavior. Heartbroken, Jane leaves the moors, and many years pass before she and Rochester are reunited.

CHAPTER 33. ADJECTIVES AND ADVERBS

Exercise 33.1, p. 307
Revising: Adjectives and adverbs

*1. The eighteenth-century essayist Samuel Johnson fared badly in his early life.
*2. Sentence correct.
*3. After failing as a schoolmaster, Johnson moved to London, where he did well.
*4. Johnson was taken seriously as a critic and dictionary maker.
*5. Johnson was really surprised when he received a pension from King George III.

6. Thinking about his meeting with the king, Johnson felt proud.
7. Sentence correct.
8. If he had been more diligent, Johnson might have made money more quickly.
9. After living cheaply for over twenty years, Johnson finally had enough money from the pension to eat and dress well.
10. With the pension, Johnson could spend time writing and live stylishly.

Exercise 33.2, p. 310
Revising: Double negatives

*1. Interest in books about the founding of the United States is not [or is hardly] consistent among Americans: it seems to vary with the national mood.

*2. Sentence correct.

3. However, when Americans <u>can</u> hardly [*or* can't] agree on major issues, sales of books about <u>the</u> Revolutionary War era increase.

4. During such periods, one cannot go to <u>any</u> bookstore without seeing several new volumes about John <u>Adams</u>, Thomas Jefferson, and other founders.

5. When Americans feel they <u>have nothing</u> [*or* don't have anything] in common, their increased interest in the early leaders may reflect a desire for unity.

Exercise 33.3, p. 312
Revising: Present and past participles

*1. Several critics found Alice Walker's *The Color Purple* to be a <u>fascinating</u> book.

*2. Sentence correct.

3. Another critic argued that although the book contained many <u>depressing</u> episodes, the overall effect was <u>exciting</u>.

4. Since other readers found the book <u>annoying</u>, this critic pointed out its many surprising [correct] qualities.

5. In the end most critics agreed that the book was a <u>satisfying</u> novel about the struggles of an African American woman.

Exercise 33.4, p. 316
Revising: Articles

*From <u>the</u> native American Indians who migrated from Asia 20,000 years ago to <u>the</u> new arrivals who now come by <u>planes</u>, <u>the</u> United States is <u>a</u> nation of foreigners. *It is <u>a</u> country of immigrants who are all living under <u>a</u> single flag.

*Back in <u>the</u> seventeenth and eighteenth centuries, at least 75 percent of <u>the</u> population came from <u>England</u>. *However, between 1820 and 1975 more than 38 million immigrants came to this country from elsewhere <u>in</u> Europe. Many children of <u>the</u> immigrants were self-conscious and <u>denied</u> their heritage; many even refused to learn <u>the</u> native language of their parents and grandparents. They tried to "Americanize" themselves. The so-called Melting Pot theory of <u>social</u> change stressed <u>the</u> importance of blending everyone together into <u>a</u> kind of stew. Each nationality would contribute its own flavor, but <u>the</u> final stew would be something called "American."

This Melting Pot theory was never completely successful. In the last half of the twentieth century, an ethnic revival changed the metaphor. Many people now see American society as a mosaic. Americans are once again proud of their heritage, and ethnic differences make the mosaic colorful and interesting.

Exercise 33.5, p. 317
Revising: Adjectives and adverbs

*1. Americans often argue about which professional sport is best: basketball, football, or baseball.
*2. Basketball fans contend that their sport offers more action because the players are constantly running and shooting.
*3. Because it is played indoors in relatively small arenas, basketball allows fans to be closer to the action than the other sports do.
*4. Football fanatics say they hardly stop yelling once the game begins.
*5. They cheer when their team executes a really complicated play well.

6. They roar more loudly when the defense stops the opponents in a goal-line stand.
7. Sentence correct.
8. In contrast, the supporters of baseball believe that it might be the perfect sport.
9. It combines the one-on-one duel of pitcher and batter struggling valiantly with the tight teamwork of double and triple plays.
10. Because the game is played slowly and carefully, fans can analyze and discuss the manager's strategy.

CHAPTER 34. MISPLACED AND DANGLING MODIFIERS

Exercise 34.1, p. 322
Revising: Misplaced modifiers

*1. People who are right-handed dominate in our society.
*2. Hand tools, machines, and even doors are designed for right-handed people.
*3. However, nearly 15 percent of the population may be left-handed.
*4. When they begin school, children often prefer one hand or the other.

*5. Parents and teachers should not try <u>deliberately</u> to change a child's preference for the left hand.

6. Women have contributed much <u>of great value</u> to American culture.

7. For example, <u>during the colonial era</u> Elizabeth Pinckney introduced indigo, the source of a valuable blue dye.

8. <u>In 1821</u> Emma Willard founded the Troy Female Seminary, the first institution to provide a college-level education for women.

9. Mary Lyon founded Mount Holyoke Female Seminary as the first true women's college with <u>a campus and directors</u> who would sustain the college even after Lyon's death.

10. *Una*, <u>which was founded by Pauline Wright Davis in 1853</u>, was the first US newspaper that was dedicated to gaining women's rights.

11. Mitchell's Comet, <u>which was named for Maria Mitchell</u>, was discovered in 1847.

12. Mitchell, <u>who lived from 1818 to 1889</u>, was the first American woman astronomer.

13. She was a member <u>of the first faculty</u> at Vassar College.

14. When elected to the <u>American Academy of Arts and Sciences in 1848</u>, she was the first woman to join the prestigious organization.

15. <u>When asked about her many accomplishments</u>, Mitchell said that she was persistent rather than especially capable.

Exercise 34.2, p. 322
Arranging adjectives

*1. A <u>young Chinese computer</u> specialist developed image controls.

*2. A <u>skeptical American</u> engineer assisted the specialist.

*3. Several <u>university</u> researchers are carrying out further study.

*4. The controls depend on <u>a hand-sized, T-shaped</u> object connected by wires to the computer.

*5. The image allows a biochemist to walk into <u>a gigantic holographic</u> display of a molecule.

6. Using <u>simple hand</u> gestures, the biochemist can rotate and change the entire image.

7. <u>All computer video</u> games also depend on computer graphics.

8. Even <u>sophisticated flight simulation</u> games operate this way.

9. One game is played with <u>two thin rectangular</u> racquets.

10. In the early years of computers, scientists made <u>some crude animated</u> drawings to simulate motion.

Exercise 34.3, p. 324
Revising: Dangling modifiers

Possible answers

*1. After Andrew Jackson had accomplished many deeds of valor, <u>his</u> fame led to his election to the presidency in 1828 and 1832.
*2. When Jackson was fourteen, both of <u>his</u> parents died.
*3. To aid the American Revolution, <u>Jackson chose</u> service as a mounted courier.
*4. Sentence correct.
*5. Though not well educated, <u>Jackson proved his ability in</u> a successful career as a lawyer and judge.

6. Because <u>Jackson won</u> many military battles, the American public believed in <u>his</u> leadership.
7. Earning the nicknames "Old Hickory" and "Sharp Knife," <u>Jackson established his military prowess</u> in the War of 1812.
8. Losing only six dead and ten wounded, the <u>triumphant Battle of New Orleans</u> burnished Jackson's reputation.
9. Jackson's victories <u>over raiding parties from Florida</u> helped pressure Spain to cede that territory.
10. While briefly governor of Florida, <u>Jackson set the US presidency as his goal.</u>

CHAPTER 35. SENTENCE FRAGMENTS

Exercise 35.1, p. 330
Revising: Sentence fragments

Possible answers

*1. Human beings who perfume themselves <u>are</u> not much different from other animals.
*2. Animals as varied as insects and dogs release <u>pheromones,</u> chemicals that signal other animals.
*3. Human beings have a diminished sense of <u>smell and</u> do not consciously detect most of their own species' pheromones.

*4. No sentence fragment.
*5. Some sources say that people began using perfume to cover up the smell of burning flesh during sacrifices to the gods.
6. No sentence fragment.
7. The earliest historical documents from the Middle East record the use of fragrances, not only in religious ceremonies but on the body.
8. In the nineteenth century, chemists began synthesizing perfume oils, which previously could be made only from natural sources.
9. The most popular animal oil for perfume today is musk, although some people dislike its heavy, sweet odor.
10. Synthetic musk oil would help conserve a certain species of deer whose gland is the source of musk.

Exercise 35.2, p. 331
Revising: Sentence fragments

Possible answers

*People generally avoid eating mushrooms except those they buy in stores. *But in fact many varieties of mushrooms are edible. *Mushrooms are members of a large group of vegetation called nonflowering plants, including algae, mosses, ferns, and coniferous trees, even the giant redwoods of California. *Most of the nonflowering plants prefer moist environments such as forest floors, fallen timber, and still water. *Mushrooms, for example, prefer moist, shady soil. *Algae grow in water.

Most mushrooms, both edible and inedible, are members of a class called basidium fungi, a term referring to their method of reproduction. The basidia produce spores, which can develop into mushrooms. This classification includes the prized meadow mushroom, cultivated commercially, and the amanitas. The amanita group contains both edible and poisonous species. Another familiar group of mushrooms, the puffballs, are easily identified by their round shape. Their spores are contained under a thick skin, which eventually ruptures to release the spores. The famous morels are in still another group. These pitted, spongy mushrooms are called sac fungi because the spores develop in sacs.

Anyone interested in mushrooms as food should heed the US Public Health Service warning not to eat any wild mushrooms unless their identity and edibility are established without a doubt.

CHAPTER 36. COMMA SPLICES AND FUSED SENTENCES

Exercise 36.1, p. 336
Sentence combining to avoid comma splices and fused sentences

Possible answers

*1. Some people think that dinosaurs were the first living vertebrates, but fossils of turtles go back 40 million years further.

*2. Although most other reptiles exist mainly in tropical regions, turtles inhabit a variety of environments worldwide.

*3. Turtles do not have teeth; their jaws are covered with a sharp, horny sheath.

*4. Turtles cannot expand their lungs to breathe air; as a result, they make adjustments in how space is used within the shell.

*5. Some turtles can get oxygen from water; therefore, they don't need to breathe air.

6. The exact origin of paper money is unknown because it has not survived as coins, shells, and other durable objects have.

7. Although scholars disagree over where paper money originated, many believe it was first used in Europe.

8. Perhaps goldsmiths were also bankers; thus they held the gold of their wealthy customers.

9. The goldsmiths probably gave customers receipts for their gold, and these receipts were then used in trade.

10. The goldsmiths were something like modern-day bankers; their receipts were something like modern-day money.

11. The goldsmiths became even more like modern-day bankers when they began issuing receipts for more gold than they actually held in their vaults.

12. Today's bankers owe more to their customers than they actually have in reserve; however, they keep enough assets on hand to meet reasonable withdrawals.

13. In economic crises, bank customers sometimes fear the loss of their money; consequently, they demand their deposits.

14. Depositors' demands may exceed a bank's reserves, and the bank may collapse.

15. The government now regulates banks to protect depositors; consequently, bank failures are less frequent than they once were.

Exercise 36.2, p. 337
Revising: Comma splices and fused sentences

Possible answers

*1. Money has a long history. It goes back at least as far as the earliest
     records.

     Money has a long history; it goes back at least as far as the earliest
     records.

*2. Many of the earliest records concern financial transactions. Indeed,
     early history must often be inferred from commercial activity.

     Many of the earliest records concern financial transactions; indeed,
     early history must often be inferred from commercial activity.

*3. Sentence correct.

*4. Sometimes the objects have had real value; however, in modern
     times their value has been more abstract.

     Although sometimes the objects have had real value, in modern
     times their value has been more abstract.

*5. Cattle, fermented beverages, and rare shells have served as money,
     and each one had actual value for the society.

     Cattle, fermented beverages, and rare shells have served as money.
     Each one had actual value for the society.

6.   As money, these objects acquired additional value because they
     represented other goods.

     As money, these objects acquired additional value; they represented
     other goods.

7.   Today money may be made of worthless paper, or it may even
     consist of a bit of data in a computer's memory.

     Today money may be made of worthless paper. It may even consist
     of a bit of data in a computer's memory.

8.   We think of money as valuable, but only our common faith in it
     makes it valuable.

     Although we think of money as valuable, only our common faith in
     it makes it valuable.

9.   That faith is sometimes fragile; consequently, currencies themselves
     are fragile.

     That faith is sometimes fragile. Consequently, currencies themselves
     are fragile.

10. Economic crises often shake the belief in money; indeed, such
    weakened faith helped cause the Great Depression of the 1930s.
    Economic crises often shake the belief in money. Indeed, such
    weakened faith helped cause the Great Depression of the 1930s.

11. Throughout history money and religion were closely linked, for
    there was little distinction between government and religion.
    Throughout history money and religion were closely linked because
    there was little distinction between government and religion.

12. Sentence correct.

13. These powerful leaders decided what objects would serve as money,
    and their backing encouraged public faith in the money.
    These powerful leaders decided what objects would serve as money.
    Their backing encouraged public faith in the money.

14. If coins were minted of precious metals, the religious overtones of
    money were then strengthened.
    Coins were minted of precious metals; the religious overtones of
    money were then strengthened.

15. Because people already believed the precious metals to be divine,
    their use in money intensified its allure.
    People already believed the precious metals to be divine; thus their
    use in money intensified its allure.

Exercise 36.3, p. 338
Revising: Comma splices and fused sentences

Possible answers

    *What many call the first genocide of modern times occurred during
World War I, when the Armenians were deported from their homes in
Anatolia, Turkey. *The Turkish government assumed that the Armenians
were sympathetic to Russia, with whom the Turks were at war. *Many
Armenians died because of the hardships of the journey, and many were
massacred. *The death toll was estimated at between 600,000 and 1 million.

    Many of the deported Armenians migrated to Russia. In 1918 they
established the Republic of Armenia, but they continued to be attacked
by Turkey. In 1920 they became the Soviet Republic of Armenia rather
than surrender to the Turks. Like other Soviet republics, Armenia became
independent in 1991. About 3.4 million Armenians live there now.

    The Armenians have a long history of conquest by others. As a people,
they formed a centralized state in the seventh century BC. Then they were
ruled by the Persian empire until it was conquered by Alexander the

Great. Greek and Roman rule followed; internal clan leadership marked by disunity and strife was next. In AD 640 the country was invaded by the Arabs. In the eleventh century it was conquered by the Byzantines and then by the Turks, under whose control it remained.

Conflict for the Armenians continues. Armenia has territorial disputes with its neighbor Azerbaijan, where many Armenians have settled.

CHAPTER 37. MIXED SENTENCES

Exercise 37.1, p. 341
Revising: Mixed sentences

Possible answers

*1. A hurricane occurs when the winds in a tropical depression rotate counterclockwise at more than seventy-four miles per hour.
*2. Because hurricanes can destroy so many lives and so much property, people fear them.
*3. Through high winds, storm surge, floods, and tornadoes, hurricanes have killed thousands of people.
*4. Storm surge occurs when the hurricane's winds whip up a tide that spills over seawalls and deluges coastal islands.
*5. Sentence correct.

6. Many scientists observe that hurricanes in recent years have become more ferocious and destructive.
7. However, in the last half-century, with improved communication systems and weather satellites, hurricanes have become less deadly.
8. The reason is that people have more time to escape.
9. Evacuation is in fact the best way for people to avoid a hurricane's force.
10. Sentence correct.

Exercise 37.2, p. 343
Revising: Repeated subjects and other parts

*1. Archaeologists and other scientists can often determine the age of their discoveries by means of radiocarbon dating.
*2. This technique can be used on any material that once was living.
*3. This technique is based on the fact that all living organisms contain carbon.

*4. The most common isotope is carbon 12, which contains six protons and six neutrons.

*5. A few carbon atoms are classified as the isotope carbon 14, where the nucleus consists of six protons and eight neutrons.

6. Because of the extra neutrons, the carbon 14 atom is unstable and radioactive.

7. Sentence correct.

8. Scientists measure the proportion of carbon 14 to carbon 12 and estimate the age of the specimen.

9. This kind of dating is most accurate when a specimen is between 500 and 50,000 years old.

10. With younger specimens too little carbon 14 has decayed, and with older ones too little is left that the scientists can measure.

5. Punctuation

CHAPTER 38. END PUNCTUATION

Exercise 38.1, p. 348
Revising: End punctuation

*When visitors first arrive in Hawaii, they often encounter an unexpected language barrier. *Standard English is the language of business and government, but many of the people speak Pidgin English. *Instead of an excited "Aloha!" the visitors may be greeted with an excited Pidgin "Howzit!" or asked if they know "how fo' find one good hotel." Many Hawaiians question whether Pidgin will hold children back because it prevents communication with *haoles,* or Caucasians, who run businesses. Yet many others feel that Pidgin is a last defense of ethnic diversity on the islands. To those who want to make standard English the official language of the state, these Hawaiians may respond, "Just 'cause I speak Pidgin no mean I dumb." They may ask, "Why you no listen?" or, in standard English, "Why don't you listen?"

CHAPTER 39. THE COMMA

Exercise 39.1, p. 351
Punctuating linked main clauses

*1. Parents once automatically gave their children the father's last name, but some no longer do.
*2. Parents were once legally required to give their children the father's last name, but these laws have been contested in court.
*3. Parents may now give their children any last name they choose, and the arguments for choosing the mother's last name are often strong and convincing.
*4. Sentence correct.
*5. The child's last name may be just the mother's, or it may link the mother's and the father's with a hyphen.

6. Sometimes the first and third children will have the mother's last name, and the second child will have the father's.
7. Occasionally, the mother and father combine parts of their names, and a new last name is formed.
8. Sentence correct.
9. Sentence correct.
10. Hyphenated names are awkward and difficult to pass on, so some observers think they will die out in a generation or two.

Exercise 39.2, p. 353
Punctuating introductory elements

*1. Veering sharply to the right, a large flock of birds neatly avoids a high wall.
*2. Sentence correct.
*3. With the help of complex computer simulations, zoologists are learning more about this movement.
*4. Because it is sudden and apparently well coordinated, the movement of flocks and schools has seemed to be directed by a leader.
*5. Almost incredibly, the group could behave with more intelligence than any individual seemed to possess.

6. However, new studies have discovered that flocks and schools are leaderless.
7. As it turns out, evading danger is really an individual response.
8. When each bird or fish senses a predator, it follows individual rules for fleeing.
9. To keep from colliding with its neighbors, each bird or fish uses other rules for dodging.
10. Multiplied over hundreds of individuals, these responses look as if they have been choreographed.

Exercise 39.3, p. 357
Punctuating essential and nonessential elements

*1. Italians insist that Marco Polo, the thirteenth-century explorer, did not import pasta from China.
*2. Pasta, which consists of flour and water and often egg, existed in Italy long before Marco Polo left for his travels.
*3. Sentence correct.

*4. Most Italians dispute this account, although their evidence is shaky.
*5. Wherever it originated, the Italians are now the undisputed masters_in making and cooking pasta.
 6. Sentence correct.
 7. Most cooks buy dried pasta, lacking the time to make their own.
 8. Sentence correct.
 9. Pasta manufacturers choose hard durum wheat_because it makes firmer cooked pasta than common wheat does.‾
 10. Pasta_made from common wheat_gets soggy in boiling water.

Exercise 39.4, p. 359
Punctuating series and coordinate adjectives

*1. Shoes with high heels were originally designed to protect feet from mud, garbage, and animal waste in the streets.
*2. Sentence correct.
*3. The heels were worn by men and made of colorful silk fabrics, soft suedes, or smooth leathers.
*4. High-heeled shoes became popular when the short, powerful King Louis XIV of France began wearing them.
*5. Louis's influence was so strong that men and women of the court, priests and cardinals, and even household servants wore high heels.
 6. Eventually only wealthy, fashionable French women wore high heels.
 7. Sentence correct.
 8. High-heeled shoes for women spread to other courts of Europe, among the Europeans of North America, and to almost all social classes.
 9. Now high heels are common, though depending on the fashion they range from short, squat, thick heels to tall, skinny spikes.
 10. Sentence correct.

Exercise 39.5, p. 364
Revising: Needless and misused commas

*1. An important source of water_is underground aquifers.
*2. Underground aquifers are deep_and sometimes broad layers of water_that are trapped between layers of rock.
*3. Porous rock_or sediment holds the water.

*4. Deep wells drilled through the top layers of solid rock_produce a flow of water.

*5. Such wells are sometimes called_artesian wells.

6. Sentence correct.

7. The Ogallala aquifer underlies a region from western Texas through northern Nebraska_and has a huge capacity of fresh water_that is contained in a layer of sand and gravel.

8. But_the water in the Ogallala is being removed at a rate faster than it is being replaced.

9. Water is pumped from the aquifer for many purposes, such as_drinking and other household use, industrial use, and_agricultural use.

10. The great plains area above the Ogallala_often lacks enough rainfall for the crops_that are grown there.

11. As a consequence, the crops in the great plains are watered by irrigation systems_that pump water from the Ogallala_and distribute it from half-mile-long sprinkler arms.

12. Scientists estimate that_at the present consumption rate the Ogallala will be depleted in forty years.

13. Sentence correct.

14. Sentence correct.

15. Without federal regulation and conservation, the Ogallala will one day_be depleted.

Exercise 39.6, p. 364
Revising: Commas

   *Ellis Island, New York, reopened for business in 1990, but now the customers are tourists, not immigrants. *This spot, which lies in New York Harbor, was the first American soil seen_or touched by many of the nation's immigrants. *Though other places also served as ports of entry for foreigners, none has the symbolic power of_Ellis Island. *Between its opening in 1892 and its closing in 1954, over 20 million people, about two-thirds of all immigrants, were detained there before taking up their new lives in the United States. *Ellis Island processed over 2000 [*or* 2,000] newcomers a day when immigration was at its peak between 1900 and 1920.

   As the end of a long voyage and the introduction to the New World, Ellis Island must have left something to be desired. The "huddled masses," as the Statue of Liberty calls them, indeed were huddled. New arrivals were herded about, kept standing in lines for hours or days, yelled at, and abused. Assigned numbers, they submitted their bodies to the pokings and proddings of the silent nurses and doctors who were charged with ferreting out the slightest sign of sickness, disability, or insanity. That test having been passed, the immigrants faced interrogation by an official through an interpreter. Those with names deemed inconveniently long or difficult to pronounce often found themselves permanently labeled with abbreviations of their names or with the names of their hometowns. But millions survived the examination, humiliation, and confusion to take the last short boat ride to New York City. For many of them and especially for their descendants, Ellis Island eventually became not a nightmare, but the place where a new life began.

CHAPTER 40. THE SEMICOLON

Exercise 40.1, p. 367
Sentence combining: Related main clauses

Possible answers

*1. Electronic instruments are prevalent in jazz and rock music; however, they are less common in classical music.

*2. Jazz and rock change rapidly; they nourish experimentation and improvisation.

*3. The notes and instrumentation of traditional classical music were established by a composer writing decades or centuries ago; therefore, such music does not change.

*4. Contemporary classical music not only can draw on tradition; it can also respond to innovations such as jazz rhythms and electronic sounds.

*5. Much contemporary electronic music is more than just jazz, rock, or classical; it is a fusion of all three.

6. Most music computers are too expensive for the average consumer; however, digital keyboard instruments can be inexpensive and are widely available.

7. Inside the keyboard is a small computer that controls a sound synthesizer; consequently, the instrument can both process and produce music.

8. The person playing the keyboard presses keys or manipulates other controls; the computer and synthesizer convert these signals into vibrations and sounds.

9. The inexpensive keyboards can perform only a few functions; still, to the novice computer musician, the range of drum rhythms and simulated instruments is exciting.
10. Would-be musicians can orchestrate whole songs from just the melody lines; they need never again play "Chopsticks."

Exercise 40.2, p. 369
Revising: Semicolons

*The set, sounds, and actors in the movie captured the essence of horror films. *The set was ideal: dark, deserted streets; trees dipping their branches over the sidewalks; mist hugging the ground and creeping up to meet the trees; looming shadows of unlighted, turreted houses. *The sounds, too, were appropriate; especially terrifying was the hard, hollow sound of footsteps echoing throughout the film. But the best feature of the movie was its actors, all of them tall, pale, and thin to the point of emaciation. With one exception, they were dressed uniformly in gray and had gray hair. The exception was an actress who dressed only in black, as if to set off her pale yellow, nearly white, long hair, the only color in the film. The glinting black eyes of another actor stole almost every scene; indeed, they were the source of the film's mischief.

CHAPTER 41. THE COLON

Exercise 41.1, p. 372
Revising: Colons and semicolons

*1. Sunlight is made up of three kinds of radiation: visible rays; infrared rays, which we cannot see; and ultraviolet rays, which are also invisible.
*2. Especially in the ultraviolet range, sunlight is harmful to the eyes.
*3. Ultraviolet rays can damage the retina; furthermore, they can cause cataracts on the lens.
*4. Infrared rays are the longest, measuring 700 nanometers and longer, while ultraviolet rays are the shortest, measuring 400 nanometers and shorter.
*5. The lens protects the eye by absorbing much of the ultraviolet radiation and thus protecting the retina.

6. By protecting the retina, however, the lens becomes a victim, growing cloudy and blocking vision.
7. The best way to protect your eyes is_to wear hats that shade the face and sunglasses that screen out the ultraviolet rays.
8. Sentence correct.
9. If sunglasses do not screen out ultraviolet rays and if people can see your eyes through them, they will not protect your eyes; and you will be at risk for cataracts later in life.
10. People who spend much time outside in the sun_really owe it to themselves to buy a pair of sunglasses that will shield their eyes.

CHAPTER 42. THE APOSTROPHE

Exercise 42.1, p. 375
Forming possessives

*1. In the myths of the ancient Greeks, the goddesses' roles vary widely.
*2. Demeter's responsibility is the fruitfulness of the earth.
*3. Athena's role is to guard the city of Athens.
*4. Artemis's function is to care for wild animals and small children.
*5. Athena and Artemis's father, Zeus, is the king of the gods.

6. Even a single goddess's responsibilities are often varied.
7. Over several centuries' time, Athena changes from a mariner's goddess to the patron of crafts.
8. Athena is also concerned with fertility and with children's well-being, since the strength of Athens depended on a large and healthy population.
9. Athena often changes into birds' forms.
10. In Homer's *Odyssey* she assumes a sea eagle's form.
11. In ancient Athens the myths of Athena were part of everyone's knowledge and life.
12. A cherished myth tells how Athena fights to retain possession of her people's land when the god Poseidon wants it.
13. Athena's and Poseidon's skills are different, and each promises a special gift to the Athenians.
14. At the contest's conclusion, Poseidon has given water and Athena has given an olive tree, for sustenance.
15. The other gods decide that the Athenians' lives depend more on Athena than on Poseidon.

Exercise 42.2, p. 377
Revising: Apostrophes

   *Landlocked Chad is among the world's most troubled countries. *The peoples of Chad are poor: their average per capita income equals $600 per year. *Just over 40 percent of Chad's population is literate, and every five hundred people must share only two teachers. The natural resources of the nation have never been plentiful, and now, as it's [correct] slowly being absorbed into the growing Sahara Desert, even water is scarce. Chad's political conflicts go back to the nineteenth century, when the French colonized the land by brutally subduing its people. The rule of the French—whose inept government of the colony did nothing to ease tensions among racial, tribal, and religious groups—ended with independence in 1960. But since then the Chadians' experience has been one of civil war and oppression, and they're also threatened with invasions from their neighbors.

CHAPTER 43. QUOTATION MARKS

Exercise 43.1, p. 382
Revising: Quotation marks

   *In one class we talked about a passage from "I Have a Dream," the speech delivered by Martin Luther King, Jr., on the steps of the Lincoln Memorial on August 28, 1963:

> *When the architects of our republic wrote the magnificent words of the Constitution and the Declaration of Independence, they were signing a promissory note to which every American was to fall heir. *This note was a promise that all men would be guaranteed the unalienable rights of life, liberty, and the pursuit of happiness.

*"What did Dr. King mean by this statement?" the teacher asked. *"Perhaps we should define 'promissory note' first." Then she explained that a person who signs such a note agrees to pay a specific sum of money on a particular date or on demand by the holder of the note. One student suggested, "Maybe Dr. King meant that the writers of the Constitution and Declaration promised that all people in America should be equal." "He and over 200,000 people had gathered in Washington, DC," added

another student. "Maybe their purpose was to demand payment, to demand those rights for African Americans." The whole discussion was an eye-opener for those of us (including me) who had never considered that those documents make promises that we should expect our country to fulfill.

CHAPTER 44. OTHER MARKS

Exercise 44.1, p. 387
Using ellipsis marks

*1. "To be able to read the Bible in the vernacular was a liberating experience. . . ."

 2. "To be able to read the Bible in the vernacular . . . freed the reader from hearing only the set passages read in the church and interpreted by the church."

 3. "Women in the sixteenth and seventeenth centuries were educated in the home and, in some cases, in boarding schools. . . . A Protestant woman was expected to read the scriptures daily, to meditate on them, and to memorize portions of them."

Exercise 44.2, p. 389
Revising: Dashes, parentheses, ellipsis marks, brackets, slashes

 *"Let all the learned say what they can, / 'Tis ready money makes the man." *These two lines of poetry by the Englishman William Somerville (1645–1742) may apply to a current American economic problem. *Non-American investors with "ready money" pour some of it—as much as $1.3 trillion in recent years—into the United States. *Stocks and bonds, savings deposits, service companies, factories, artworks, political campaigns—the investments of foreigners are varied and grow more numerous every day. Proponents of foreign investment argue that it revives industry, strengthens the economy, creates jobs (more than 3 million, they say), and encourages free trade among nations. Opponents caution that the risks associated with heavy foreign investment—namely decreased profits at home and increased political influence from outside—may ultimately weaken the economy. On both sides, it seems, "the learned say . . . / 'Tis ready money makes the man [or country]." The question is, whose money—theirs or ours?

6. Spelling and Mechanics

CHAPTER 45. SPELLING

Exercise 45.1, p. 396
Using correct spellings

*1. Science <u>affects</u> many <u>important</u> aspects of our lives.
*2. Many people have a <u>poor</u> understanding of the <u>role</u> of scientific breakthroughs in <u>their</u> health.
*3. Many people <u>believe</u> that <u>doctors</u>, more than science, are <u>responsible</u> for <u>improvements</u> in <u>health</u> care.
*4. But scientists in the <u>laboratory</u> have made crucial steps in the search for <u>knowledge</u> about <u>health</u> and <u>medicine</u>.
*5. For example, one scientist <u>whose</u> discoveries have <u>affected</u> many people is Ulf Von Euler.

6. In the 1950s Von Euler's discovery of certain hormones <u>led</u> to the invention of the birth control pill.
7. Von Euler's work was used by John Rock, who <u>developed</u> the first birth control pill and influenced family <u>planning</u>.
8. Von Euler also discovered the <u>principal</u> neurotransmitter that controls the heartbeat.
9. Another scientist, Hans Selye, showed what <u>effect</u> stress can have on the body.
10. His findings have <u>led</u> to methods of <u>bearing</u> stress.

Exercise 45.2, p. 397
Working with a spelling checker

*The <u>weather affects</u> all of us, though <u>its effects</u> are different for different people. *Some people love a <u>fair</u> day with warm temperatures and sunshine. *They revel in spending a <u>whole</u> day outside without the threat of <u>rain</u>. Other people prefer dark <u>rainy days</u>. They relish the opportunity to slow down and <u>hear their</u> inner thoughts. Most people agree, however, that <u>too</u> much of one kind of <u>weather</u>—rain, sun, snow, or clouds—makes them <u>bored</u>.

CHAPTER 46. THE HYPHEN

Exercise 46.1, p. 399
Using hyphens

*1. Sentence correct.
*2. Sentence correct.
*3. The non-African elephants of south-central Asia are somewhat smaller.
*4. A fourteen- or fifteen-year-old elephant has reached sexual maturity.
*5. The elephant life span is about sixty-five or seventy years.

6. Sentence correct.
7. It stands about thirty-three inches high.
8. A two-hundred-pound, thirty-three-inch baby is quite a big baby.
9. Unfortunately, elephants are often killed for their ivory tusks, and partly as a result they are an increasingly endangered species.
10. Sentence correct.

CHAPTER 47. CAPITAL LETTERS

Exercise 47.1, p. 403
Revising: Capitals

*1. San Antonio, Texas, is a thriving city in the Southwest.
*2. The city has always offered much to tourists interested in the roots of Spanish settlement of the New World.
*3. The Alamo is one of five Catholic missions built by priests to convert Native Americans and to maintain Spain's claims in the area.
*4. But the Alamo is more famous for being the site of an 1836 battle that helped to create the Republic of Texas.
*5. Many of the nearby streets, such as Crockett Street, are named for men who died in that battle.

6. The Hemisfair Plaza and the San Antonio River link tourist and convention facilities.
7. Restaurants, hotels, and shops line the river. The haunting melodies of "Una Paloma Blanca" and "Malagueña" lure passing tourists into Casa Rio and other Mexican restaurants.

8. The University of Texas at San Antonio has expanded, and a medical center lies in the northwest part of the city.
9. Sentence correct.
10. The city has attracted high-tech industry, creating a corridor between San Antonio and Austin.

CHAPTER 48. UNDERLINING OR ITALICS

Exercise 48.1, p. 407
Revising: Underlining or italics

*1. Of the many Vietnam veterans who are writers, Oliver Stone is perhaps the most famous for writing and directing the films Platoon and Born on the Fourth of July.
*2. Tim O'Brien has written short stories for Esquire, GQ, and Massachusetts Review.
*3. Going After Cacciato is O'Brien's dreamlike novel about the horrors of combat.
*4. The word Vietnam is technically two words (Viet and Nam), but most American writers spell it as one word. [*Viet* and *Nam* were correctly highlighted. Highlighting removed from *one*.]
*5. American writers use words or phrases borrowed from Vietnamese, such as di di mau ("go quickly") or dinky dau ("crazy").

6. Philip Caputo's gripping account of his service in Vietnam appears in the book A Rumor of War. [Highlighting removed from *gripping*.]
7. Sentence correct.
8. David Rabe's plays—including The Basic Training of Pavlo Hummel, Streamers, and Sticks and Bones—depict the effects of the war not only on the soldiers but on their families. [Highlighting removed from *not only . . . but*.]
9. Called the poet laureate of the Vietnam war, Steve Mason has published two collections of poems: Johnny's Song and Warrior for Peace. [Highlighting removed from *poet laureate of the Vietnam war*.]
10. The Washington Post published rave reviews of Veteran's Day, an autobiography by Rod Kane. [Highlighting removed from *rave*.]

CHAPTER 49. ABBREVIATIONS

Exercise 49.1, p. 411
Revising: Abbreviations

*1. Sentence correct.

*2. About 65 <u>million</u> <u>years</u> ago, a comet or asteroid crashed into the earth.

*3. The result was a huge crater about 10 <u>kilometers</u> (6.2 <u>miles</u>) deep in the Gulf of <u>Mexico</u>.

*4. Sharpton's new measurements suggest that the crater is 50 <u>percent</u> larger than scientists had previously believed.

*5. Indeed, 20-<u>year</u>-old drilling cores reveal that the crater is about 186 <u>miles</u> wide, roughly the size of <u>Connecticut</u>.

6. Sentence correct.

7. On impact, 200,000 cubic <u>kilometers</u> of rock and soil were vaporized or thrown into the air.

8. That's the equivalent of 2.34 <u>billion</u> cubic feet of matter.

9. The impact would have created <u>400-foot</u> tidal waves across the <u>Atlantic</u> Ocean, <u>temperatures</u> higher than 20,000 <u>degrees</u>, and powerful earthquakes.

10. Sharpton theorizes that the dust, vapor, and smoke from this impact blocked the sun's rays for <u>months</u>, cooled the earth, and thus resulted in the death of the dinosaurs.

CHAPTER 50. NUMBERS

Exercise 50.1, p. 413
Revising: Numbers

*1. The planet Saturn is <u>900</u> million miles, or nearly <u>1.5 billion</u> kilometers, from the sun.

*2. Sentence correct.

*3. Thus, Saturn orbits the sun only <u>2.4</u> times during the average human life span.

*4. It travels in its orbit at about <u>21,600</u> miles per hour.

*5. <u>Fifteen</u> to <u>twenty</u> times denser than Earth's core, Saturn's core measures <u>seventeen thousand</u> miles across.

6. The temperature at Saturn's cloud tops is <u>−170</u> degrees Fahrenheit.

7. In <u>1933</u>, astronomers found on Saturn's surface a huge white spot <u>two</u> times the size of Earth and <u>seven</u> times the size of Mercury.

8. Saturn's famous rings reflect almost <u>70</u> percent of the sunlight that approaches the planet.

9. The ring system is almost <u>40,000</u> miles wide, beginning 8,800 miles from the planet's visible surface and ending <u>47,000</u> miles from that surface.

10. The Cassini-Huygens spacecraft traveled more than <u>820 million</u> miles to explore and photograph Saturn.

7. Research and Documentation

CHAPTER 51. RESEARCH STRATEGY

Exercise 51.1, p. 419
Finding a subject and question

Individual response.

CHAPTER 52. FINDING SOURCES

Exercise 52.1, p. 446
Finding sources

Individual response.

CHAPTER 53. WORKING WITH SOURCES

Exercise 53.1, p. 456
Evaluating a source

Responses will vary. Packard's book is famously critical of advertising methods. Students should recognize Packard's bias while also valuing his expertise and evidence.

Exercise 53.2, p. 456
Evaluating Web sites

Individual response.

Exercise 53.3, p. 456
Evaluating a Web log

Individual response.

Exercise 53.4, p. 456
Evaluating an online discussion

Individual response.

Exercise 53.5, p. 458
Synthesizing sources

The key similarities and differences are these:

Similarities: Nadelmann and Posey agree that crackdowns or penalties do not stop the drug trade. Nadelmann and Runkle agree that the drug trade affects the young, who are most impressionable.

Differences: Nadelmann maintains that the illegal drug trade does more to entice youths to drugs than do the drugs themselves, whereas Runkle maintains that the illegality discourages youths from using prohibited drugs. Posey, in contrast to Runkle, claims that penalties do nothing to discourage drug abusers.

Students' paragraphs will depend on their views, but here is a sample response:

Posey seems to invalidate the whole debate over drug legalization: nothing, he says from experience, will stop drug abuse. But such a futile view, whatever its truth, cannot stop the search for a solution. We have tried the prohibition favored by Runkle. Even if, as she claims, students are using fewer illegal drugs, prohibition has not worked. It may be time to try the admittedly risky approach proposed by Nadelmann, legalizing drugs to "drive the drug-dealing business off the streets."

Exercise 53.6, p. 464
Summarizing and paraphrasing

Possible summary

Eisinger et al. 44
Federalism, unlike a unitary system, allows the states autonomy. Its strength and its weakness—which are in balance—lie in the regional differences it permits.

Possible paraphrase

Eisinger et al. 44
Under federalism, each state can devise its own ways of handling problems and its own laws. The system's advantage is that a state can operate according to its people's culture, morals, and wealth. A unitary system like that in France does not permit such diversity.

Exercise 53.7, p. 464
Combining summary, paraphrase, and direct quotation

Possible answer

Farb 107
Speakers at parties often "unconsciously duel" in conversations in order to assert "dominance" over others. A speaker may mumble, thus preventing a listener from understanding what is said. Or he or she may continue talking after the listener has moved away, a "challenge to the listener to return and acknowledge the dominance of the speaker."

Exercise 53.8, p. 470
Introducing and interpreting borrowed material

Sample paragraph

Why does a woman who is otherwise happy regularly suffer anxiety attacks at the first sign of spring? Why does a man who is otherwise a competent, relaxed driver feel panic whenever he approaches a traffic rotary? According to Willard Gaylin, a professor of psychiatry and a practicing psychoanalyst, such feelings of anxiety are attributable to the uniquely human capacities for remembering, imagining, and forming "symbolic and often unconscious representations" of experiences (23). The feeling of anxiety, Gaylin says, "is . . . compounded by its seemingly irrational quality": it may appear despite the absence of an immediate source of worry or pain (23). The anxious woman is not aware of it, but her father's death twenty years before in April has caused her to equate spring with death. Similarly, the man has forgotten that a terrible accident he witnessed as a child occurred at a rotary. For both people, the anxious feelings are not reduced but heightened because they seem to be unfounded.

CHAPTER 54. AVOIDING PLAGIARISM AND DOCUMENTING SOURCES

Exercise 54.1, p. 475
Recognizing plagiarism

1. Plagiarized: takes phrases directly from the original without quotation marks.
2. Acceptable.
3. Inaccurate and plagiarized: the passage uses phrases from the original without quotation marks and distorts its meaning.
4. Acceptable: puts the original into the author's own words and correctly conveys its meaning.
5. Inaccurate and plagiarized: fails to acknowledge the source and fails to convey accurately the concepts of "discrimination" and "confusing" outlined in the original.
6. Inaccurate: ellipses are needed to indicate that material was omitted, and brackets must be placed around lowercase *s* to indicate revision.

CHAPTER 56. MLA DOCUMENTATION AND FORMAT

Exercise 56.1, p. 520
Writing works-cited entries

Bridging the Digital Divide. Chicago: ALA, 2006.

Carvin, Andy. "MyPyramid.gov: Achieving E-Health for All?" Digital

   Divide Network. 22 Feb. 2005. Benton Foundation. 10 Nov.

   2006 <http://www.digitaldivide.net/articles>.

Chester, Jeff. "The Threat to the Net." Nation 9 Oct. 2005: 6-7.

   Expanded Academic ASAP. InfoTrac. Southeast State U, Polk

   Lib. 14 Nov. 2006 <http://www.galegroup.com>.

*Conte, Christopher. "Networking the Classroom." <u>CQ Researcher</u> 5

   (2005): 923-43.

*Healy, Jane M. <u>Failure to Connect: How Computers Affect Our</u>

   <u>Children's Minds—For Better and Worse</u>. New York:

   Simon, 2000.

*Irving, Larry. "The Still Yawning Divide." <u>Newsweek</u> 12 Mar. 2006: 64.

   Expanded Academic ASAP. InfoTrac. Southeast State U, Polk

   Lib. 14 Nov. 2006 <http://www.galegroup.com>.

 McArthur, Mary. E-mail interview. 31 Oct. 2006.

*United States. Dept. of Education. National Center for Education

   Statistics. <u>Internet Access in Public Schools</u>. 24 Feb. 2005. 12

   Nov. 2006 <http://www.ed.gov/nces/edstats>.